LIGHT IN THE DARKNESS

SPIRITUALLY AND PHYSICALLY PREPARING FOR FOSTER/ADOPTION

JORDAN CHESNUT

New Harbor Press

RAPID CITY, SD

Chesnut/New Harbor Press
1601 Mt. Rushmore Rd, Ste 3288
Rapid City, SD 57701
www.NewHarborPress.com

Ordering Information:
Quantity sales. Special discounts are available on quantity purchases by cor-
porations, associations, and others. For details, contact the "Special Sales
Department" at the address above.

Light in the Darkness/Jordan Chesnut —1st ed.
ISBN 978-1-63357-463-2

CONTENTS

SCULPTING CHARACTER

SOME PEOPLE VIEW LIFE as a culmination of choices that you made leading to your current place in life. Others believe in destiny. Meaning, you were going to end up where you are in life regardless of your efforts. Nothing was going to change that. If most people look back on their life, they can likely pinpoint a moment that set them on a trajectory landing them in their current situation, for better or worse.

I am convinced that we have two outcomes in life and God knows both. Our path and God's path. If you are a Christian, then you are confronted with an important reality. You already acknowledge that you are nothing without God. This does not end with baptism. You need to continue this mindset into your prayer life. What is God's calling for your life? If we are left to our own choices, we will choose wrong. The existence of sin proves this.

"Trust in the Lord with all your heart. Lean not into temptation", (Proverbs 3:5) or "Worry about nothing pray about everything", (Phil. 4:6). We are taught to use these verses to guide us through tough times. Countless people have come to realize that fully trusting in God and praying about everything can lead you in directions you never would have dreamed.

This is why many people refuse to pray for patience. In doing so God will give you the opportunity to work on patience. The truth of the matter is that spiritual obedience should lead to physical action.

This is how Christians become important assets to God's overall mission. Prayer enables God to present His will for your life. Without prayer and God's influence we make messes of our lives through human choice. Again, we are nothing without God. Human choice creates a broken lifestyle that can last generations. I call this the cycle of brokenness. Generation after generation repeats the errors of their family until Christ intervenes.

I grew up in a unique family. As a child I viewed us as "normal". With age I have learned a "normal" family does not exist. I was the youngest of three. My oldest brother was adopted at two months old. I always looked up to him and seemed to repeatedly forget he was adopted. It did not matter to me. He was my brother and taught me a lot about guitars and music, which was cool. My other brother, Justin, was diagnosed with Duchenne Muscular Dystrophy at age 9. He was born with this but was undiagnosed for years due to a lack of knowledge about the insidious disease. When I was in junior high and high school, I helped take care of him quite a bit. I helped him exercise his muscles as much as possible. This prolonged his mobility and delayed his reliance on a wheelchair.

We were best friends and virtually inseparable. Most weekends I stayed with him and hung out at his college. When he graduated, he was offered a good job and I would often drop him off at work then pick him up. He inspired me with his drive to make the most out of life and not throw a pity party for himself. I never heard him complain about having Muscular Dystrophy. When I asked him why God would give him this disease he said, "Why not me? Do you want to take it?".

His health began failing about a year later. Due to the fact the heart is a muscle, the disease started to affect it. The scariest moment of my life was a phone call from him at work asking me to get him. He wasn't feeling well. When I pulled up and loaded him in the van, he began having seizures.

With no time to strap his wheelchair in, I sped to the hospital with one hand holding him and the chair in place while he was convulsing. From that point on he was in and out of the hospital. The night before he passed, I was distraught. He was brought home by ambulance to our house to pass away. We were told he had a couple weeks left. I was trying to joke around with him a bit as a poor effort to distract from the depressing elephant lingering in the room, but he was tired and just wanted to take a nap.

I decided to play a show that night with a band I was in. When I got home, he was asleep again. In the morning he was gone. To this day I feel guilty. I should have been with him and been by his side. Instead, I was playing music in a bar.

I say all of this because it is the foundation that sculpted me into who I am today. It was from this point I started making different decisions with my life. We only have a short time on Earth. Our time can be used selfishly or to glorify God. Once character is cultivated and given back to the Lord, a foundation is established that can go beyond personal salvation and be transitioned towards kingdom building.

After my brother passed away it was a weird feeling not being needed. I experienced a transfer from action into character at this point. Did I help Justin because I needed to, or because I wanted to? This was a defining character trait I learned about myself. I missed helping. I had a desire to give back.

This desire to help is ultimately what led my wife Rae and I to adoption. It takes specific people to adopt children. Adopting a child requires dedication, sacrifice, and nerve. It requires a foundation that has cultivated a person who wants to help others and give back. What makes you want to give more and why? As of this writing, there are over 450,000 children in foster care within the United States and over 100,000 of those children are eligible for and waiting to be adopted. Does this number make you simply feel sad, or does it make you want to do something? (Sosiladmin, 2022)

Biblical Reflection

Faith in Action

James 2:20-22 - *"You foolish person, do you want evidence that faith without deeds is useless? Was not our father Abraham considered righteous for what he did when he offered his son Isaac on the altar? You see that his faith and his actions were working together, and his faith was made complete by what he did."*

When reflecting on God's call for our life we need to remove society and tradition from our thoughts. We need to look clearly at what the Bible says. It is not enough that our heart goes out to regrettable things that occur. What are Christians going to do about it?

Abraham trusted God fully. To test Abraham's loyalty and to show the character of the one true God, He asked for a pagan style sacrifice. Abraham followed God even in this path. God saw Abraham's loyalty and showed him His true character. The true God we serve is the Creator of life, not destroyer. The God we serve is love.

God has placed you in a position to build His kingdom. How is He calling you to do that? Are you stepping into the doors He is opening for you?

_____

_____

_____

_____

_____

_____

Prayer

Lord, give me guidance into the ministry you are calling me to. Show me your will for my life and help me develop the character I need to fulfill your mission and calling for my life. -Amen

Marriage and a Baby Carriage

WHEN PEOPLE MARRY THE inevitable conversation is discussed regarding how long to wait before trying for children. My conversation was different. Rae and I had always thought we should adopt. The transfer of this to prayer had not happened yet. When we got married, I was 22 and Rae was 19. We would have been young to have children as it was. We had just bought a house and were both in college working 2-4 jobs each. Once we settled into our chosen fields and started making some money we began to talk about kids.

The question of whether we should adopt first or try to have a biological child was discussed, but to be honest I'm not sure how much we prayed about God's will. I just remember us deciding if we couldn't get pregnant then we should adopt. Logical, right? After about 2 years we finally got pregnant. We were excited and giddy about having a baby. Our joy faded when the ultrasound showed our baby had stopped growing. I was devastated and Rae was a mess. I felt like a failure and was filled with guilt. I had led us in a significant life choice based off what society did and not prayer. We had felt a pull towards adoption and decided to try for a baby without praying through that feeling to see what God was trying to tell us.

The miscarriage did not happen naturally. After a month Rae needed to have a D&C. The depressing feelings I had were only worsened by the fact I had to fill out a Death Certificate before surgery.

Those feelings quickly led to frustration as it occurred to me that I was filling out a Death Certificate before a procedure to remove our baby that passed away when somewhere someone was having the same procedure to remove a healthy one because she did not want it. All I wanted to do was throw up at the thought. We named our baby Gabriel. The meaning of the name is "things yet to come".

It took a long time to heal from this. Being around babies after losing one was tough. Looking at babies that would have been our baby's age caused us to have a sick feeling in our stomachs. After a little healing took place, we decided to look toward adoption.

We first began looking into adoption within the United States. The waiting list is a bit overwhelming and trying to find an agency to go with was very confusing. So, we started looking at overseas adoption.

Agencies were not hard to find on this route. We quickly realized the expenses that would be incurred in that venture. Most countries required $30,000-$40,000 total cost for adoption. The thought of this frustrated us. I started calculating how to do this. I figured if I sold my car and just bought a beater with a heater, then lived off one paycheck for a while, we could get there. After mapping out that time frame in conjunction with these numbers it wasn't long until I just got mad.

It costs less than $1000 for an abortion and the procedure has even been transformed into a pill to avoid surgery at times, but to give a child a loving home once they are born is 30-40 times that. I could fume all day about it but what could we do? The idea of putting ourselves in such a tight financial place this early in our marriage seemed irresponsible. We had only been married for about five years and were still paying on my student loans. Furthermore, Rae had just bought a business.

As reality confronted us, our sights turned toward foster care. This step petrified us. The idea that we could have a child in our house who might go back to the home they were pulled from was unthinkable to us. How would we be able to let a child go back to a home that was so troubled? Add to that, we just lost a baby. Could we take more loss? We were terrified at these thoughts. These steps were going to take us into the unknown. It was nerve-racking, but I knew it was what God was calling us to.

Rae and I had little to worry about. We were enjoying life until having problems starting a family. The choice of whether to talk with someone about becoming foster parents had me feeling guilty again. I began to think about why we were doing this. Had I prayed with Rae about this a year and a half ago she may not be so sad and depressed. I was trying to make things right and needed to take the lead on this.

Growing up I saw my dad work his tail off and mom take care of us kids. In my mind fathers worked and on rare occasions raised their voices to "lay down the law". I followed his footsteps and took the natural steps of life. God had different plans and I hadn't checked with him. The process Rae and I went through brought us to prayer and a close listening distance to God. It was terrifying. People talk about wanting to get close to God. Some people fail to do this out of fear of what He may ask you to do.

After fully knowing foster care was what God was asking of us, I picked up the phone and a foster agency representative came to our house to talk. Rae was just following along at this point. I'm not sure she was quite ready for children. Taking the initiative without knowing exactly what Rae was thinking left me unsettled, but I knew it was what we were supposed to do. It was the first time I started to blindly follow God and pray he would take care of us. When looking at the term "head of the household" it is important to realize the Biblical meaning. Fulfilling that term means you are responsible for being the spiritual leader of your family. It is an enormous responsibility, and it starts with prayer.

Biblical Reflection

Waiting on the Lord

Psalm 46:10 "Be still, and know that I am God."

Do not fall into the trap of trying to force God's will. In doing so you may be going against His will. This is where prayer is important. We cannot fulfill God's will without prayer. Prayer is the only line of communication to God. The Bible is our guideline and example of God's character. God's will for our lives is found through prayer. Without prayer we are making human choices rather than following divine will. Wait and be patient. God is in control, and we follow his schedule, not our own.

What are areas of your life that you may be neglecting in prayer? What are some concerns that you need to bring to the Lord? Is there something that you may be pushing that God wants you to wait on?

_____

_____

_____

_____

_____

_____

Prayer

Heavenly father, help me understand that you are all knowing. You are the Creator of all things and have a plan that is based on your timing and not mine. Help me to be patient in your glorious plan. -Amen

THE JOURNEY TO FOSTER CARE

OUR HOUSE HAD TWO bedrooms and one bathroom bringing the little bungalow to 1058 square feet. We stated to our foster agency that we were looking for one child. They told us we could be licensed for two children with our house, and we should just register for two in case we changed our minds and wanted two siblings. The thought of that petrified me. In my mind I was thinking our life was hectic enough without two children in the mix. I was just wanting one well-behaved child. I decided not to worry much about the advice, and we registered our house to accept up to two children.

Our next step in this venture was foster care training. This was an eye opener. The wide variety of people who attended these meetings was breathtaking. Some were clearly in it for the wrong reasons and others seemed to be in the same situation as us. There was an additional couple that seemed to look at foster care as a ministry field and wanted to make a difference in children's lives, which was admirable. Most of them had a desire to take on a child up to the age of 3. We stated we would take a child up to the age of 9. We did not want a baby at this point.

What caught my attention through the training was traveling the course of what a child learns. If a child never has a parent come to their aid when they fall, then they will learn to never scream for help. This thought process went deep in conversation. The other helpful hints we received brought attention to the ways we could help children feel comfortable when they come to our home. If you do not decorate your child's room ahead of their arrival and allow them to choose colors or posters it can help the transition. This is also something that you are doing together that will naturally create conversation. Letting them have input in the process is something many foster children do not have. These children were pulled from their home with no choice and placed in a foster home with no choice. Any chance to give foster children choices builds relationships and trust.

After three Saturdays of training and a file cabinet drawer of paperwork completed, we were licensed foster parents. The day we received our license in the mail we also answered a phone call. It was for a girl and boy. This placement was for respite care. Basically, a foster mom needed a break from her children, and they called us to watch them temporarily. Rae and I thought it would be a good trial to see how well we could handle two children. I had mixed feelings about the prospect. However, if she was getting on board and happy about it, I needed to support that.

We were nervous wondering what to expect. Were they going to come to our house and break everything? Did I need to lock my guitar collection up? Will they scream constantly until their foster mom comes back? There were endless unanswered questions that petrified me.

When they came to our house, they were the cutest children you could have met. Quickly, I thought we had the most perfect children staying at our house. *Could we just keep these two?* Rae and I were playing house, for real, and it was a blast. When we got them to sleep, and we were getting around for bed I thought; *we aren't too bad at this! The house wasn't on fire and the kids were quiet. This isn't bad!*

After a week reality set in. The girl got a piece of straw stuck deep inside her ear, which almost resulted in a hospital visit. The boy had trauma that caused him never to cry, though we knew he had to be hurt at times. His reflexes were slow, and he was always falling or bumping into things. This made me a nervous wreck.

We found out later that no one ever picked him up when he cried, as was discussed in foster training. He missed important early development stages. He had never had any personal interaction, thus preventing him from properly learning fine motor skills. We just never knew if he was hurt or not. Several more days and flamboyant temper tantrums from the girl, we felt like we earned our own vacation.

Those children left on Friday. Before we had time to think, we received three phone calls for placements that weekend. Those phone calls are the most on the spot stressful choices to make, ever. In a split second you can change your life forever. The thoughts were swarming in the back of our minds. Is this what God wants us to do? You don't exactly have time for a spiritual retreat to pray and seek God's leading on the matter during the phone call. We were taught in foster training to have our questions ready.

Our questions were, "Are they legal risk?" Meaning, have the parents already had rights terminated on previous children. This meant they were less likely to go back to their birth home. "Are there any mental disorders we should know about?" "What are their ages?" "Tell us about them."

The problem with these phone calls is the desperation of the person on the other line. They are trying hard to find someone to take these children. So, if you aren't taking the child(ren); they need to quickly get off the phone and make another call. These agencies work on efficiency. The quicker they place a child the better their agency ranks. This can play a role in their funding. This also means full information is not always given. If you know too much you may not take the child(ren).

Always have those questions ready. These are life altering choices to make. If a child comes to your house and it does not work out the child is affected long-term. If you feel obligated to keep this child your life is altered, perhaps negatively. There is no "perfect match". To assume so means that you as an individual are perfect. No one is perfect. There are no magic words or actions that will make your child the image you have in your head. A biological child will never meet that image either. You just perceive it differently because they are part of you; and again, you are not perfect.

Going into foster care or adoption will force parents to confront this reality. You know your problems and shortcomings. You do not know the child's troubles fully until they are presented. Prayer and guidance are needed to bridge the gap. This is where adoption transitions to a mission field.

BIBLICAL REFLECTION

Spiritual Warfare

1 Peter 5:8 "Be alert and of sober mind. Your enemy the devil prowls around like a roaring lion looking for someone to devour."

IF YOU HAVE EVER been hunting for food, you will quickly learn something. The animal you are likely to get is the one that makes a mistake. It is the one that stops focusing when danger is close by. Your meal is the animal that is distracted. This is what the "lion" Satan is looking for. Satan will attack you in your weakest moments.

When you bring a child into your home to foster or adopt, they have typically come from a home where God has been vacant from the equation. It is important to look at this in the same manner as a ministry field. You will see resistance as with any ministry field. Stay focused on God's work. Remain in close prayer to your protector. Put on the full armor of God.

Foster/adoption should be a calling from God. If you adopt a child into your home and introduce Christianity to them, expect spiritual resistance. This is a subject that can make people squeamish. Many church denominations will also resist some of these notions. The reality is that "We battle not against flesh and blood but the prince and principalities of the air" (Ephesians 6:12).

Not only is this a widely dismissed concept in the Bible, but it is seldom studied with intensity when adopting children. If Christians adopt a child and introduce them to Christ, a spiritual battle will occur in their house.

Satan has dominion over the earth. As a result, your child was likely in a situation where Satan had a stronghold on their prior home. As a Christian, you cannot be naïve to the notion that this will transfer into your home. If you are making spiritual progress in your child do not neglect this possibility, be alert. Do not set your calling from God up for failure. Pray through every aspect of your house and family. Be fervent. Satan comes to the weak. If you are weak in this awareness, then Satan will attack you there.

To put this into perspective, up to 80 percent of foster children have significant mental health issues compared to 18 to 22 percent of the regular population (childwelfare.gov, 2023). With fewer home placements, mental and physical health problems drop significantly (psychiatry.org, 2023). The more placements a child has, the more likely they are to have fears of stability. This can lead to delayed permanency, aggression, depression, educational delays, and more (Casey, 2023). Be aware of the mental and spiritual side-effects of a child in your care. I believe many times the symptoms overlap.

This can be a strange concept for some Christians. We live in an increasingly secular society that has even worked its way into common Christian practices. Many Christians are forced to neglect talking about spiritual issues at work to insure their employment. Many churches neglect the subject in many settings to avoid alienating new people coming to services. This has helped to create an atmosphere that makes it taboo to speak about and address the spiritual warfare that is very much at work in this temporary world.

Do not neglect this subject. If we believe the Bible to be a true message from God, then we need to take it seriously and transfer those practices into our daily lives. We cannot hide from spiritual warfare. It will become a thorn in our lives, or we can confront it with Christ.

Are you preparing spiritually for your mission? Are you apprehensive about spiritual warfare? Why?

_____

_____

_____

_____

_____

_____

Prayer-

Holy Spirit give me the strength and wisdom to do the work of Jesus Christ. Make me aware of the enemy's plans. Help me navigate through them and provide a Christian environment that will foster a closer relationship with you as a family unit. -Amen

The Placement

WE ACCEPTED PLACEMENT FOR two boys. I must admit the thought of having two boys was nerve-racking. At first, I was talking to Rae about holding out for one child. After discussing it we decided the odds of getting called for just one child were going to be slim. Most of the time parents have at least one or two children before abuse is noticed and family services are contacted. For example, an older child is already in school when teachers notice bruises, or a neighbor notices children running around for hours while not being supervised.

Only after people report an issue will family services investigate. Typically, what happens is a process of encouraging parents to be more responsible and requiring them to take classes. It can take a long time before children are pulled from a home. The thought of getting a call for just one older child seemed unlikely.

With some prayer and consideration, we decided to accept these two boys. We were told they were a little wild and that was why they were being moved. While this was not the best thing to hear, it also came to our attention the foster parents they currently had were not the best fit either. The blessing of this placement was having two weeks to prepare for them, which was rare. Most of the time placement occurs very quickly. A child is taken into care, and they need a home immediately. The idea of being able to mentally prepare and get the house ready was great. Plus, we had a day or two to give them an answer on taking the children or not. We requested some information on what the boys were interested in and decorated the room with their favorite superheroes.

Yes, foster training said let the kids help decorate. However, we thought it would be less stressful to avoid a two and five-year-old helping paint their room. Rae and her friends painted a wall to look like Gotham City and put super-heroes on the walls. My dad helped me build a bunk bed. Having support when you are looking into foster care or adoption is a must! Supportive friends and family are the backbone of your mental stability. You will need them to vent, bounce ideas off, and take the kids for an hour or two while you get a brief recharge.

After a couple of "last hoorah" celebratory date nights to our end of freedom; we had two boys in our home. The boys were visibly overwhelmed from moving. Meanwhile, they were adjusting to where they would be living. As they looked at their room, they looked a little stunned and did not know what to think.

It is easy, as a parent, to have everything "perfect" and have this picture in your head of how you want things to go. Or what you hope their personalities will be like. The reality is we were our kid's fourth home (placement) in eleven months. They were not going to try to attach to us.

The first two weeks were amazing! We were waiting for the honeymoon to be over; and dreading it. There are always grace periods in foster children, and we were ready for the switch to flip. Behaviors can be good for a period, like tolerating a bold personality at family Thanksgiving dinner. You simply bite your tongue until the meal is done.

Given time, everyone shows who they are. The problem was we were not sure how long this would take. At week three we questioned if it was going to happen. Week four passed and I determined we simply got lucky and had great kids. One month and a week solidified my thoughts. A month and a half came, and the eye opener occurred.

We were at Walmart and our five-year-old was touching absolutely everything in sight. I corrected him repeatedly and he started purposely disobeying me and knocking things off the shelves. I gave him a glare and he dropped to the floor dragging things off the shelf. I told him, "That's it, Rae is staying with your brother, and we are going to the car". At this point he started throwing a temper tantrum. I tried to take his hand and gently lead him out to the car. That was a joke. The kicking and screaming started. I picked him up and he started yelling at the top of his lungs, "Please don't take me to the car! Please don't take me to the car!" about twenty times before we reached the door. The looks I received the whole way were so judgmental and condemning, I was mortified.

During that pleasant stroll I was thinking about those looks. They had no clue what was going on. Simultaneously, I was wondering what had happened to him in the car before. Was it just a swat? Probably not.

Once we arrived at the car, I put him in the back seat and closed the door. I got in the driver's seat and said nothing. I have found if you have no clue what to do in a situation, nothing is typically the best response. I had no idea what was going through his mind. He also had no clue that I was going to leave him alone. I wanted him to know I was not going to abuse him in any way. I figured the best way to accomplish that task was by doing nothing.

Five minutes later he settled down. I asked, "Have I spanked you?" He shook his head no. "Have I hurt you?" He again shook his head no. "I asked you to keep your hands to yourself in the store and to stop touching things. You disrespected me and didn't listen. In our house if Rae or I ask you to do something, you do it. We are adults and you are a kid. You listen to adults. Because you did not listen, and you were making a mess. I needed to take you out of the store. You kicked and screamed the whole way to the car. I am guessing someone hit you or spanked you in the car before. I won't do that. Next time if I ask you to do something, just listen."

* * *

I am an advocate that everyone requires a tailored form of discipline. For several years I substituted in schools in one capacity or another. During this time, I learned that some children naturally want to behave and please authority figures. Some just want to know what they can get away with. Until you have figured this out, being extremely strict is not always the best method. It can cause a child to quickly despise you. This creates a trust barrier that can be hard to overcome. Try to figure out what kind of child you are raising and start small with discipline.

Work out a reward and punishment form of discipline. I could be judged by psychologists for saying "punishment". However, I believe avoiding the use of the word punishment is side stepping the reality of what happens as an adult. Prepare your kids for reality. Let your child know what you ALWAYS expect. Be consistent and have a discipline that directly relates to the offense. If they break something explain what it cost and have them work that off by cleaning up the baseboards, windows, etc. Put yourself in their shoes. Find out what will reach them.

Reaching them is key. Each of our children respond differently to timeout. I heard an interesting perspective on putting your children in timeout from Pastor Alex Seeley. Her belief is that timeout is not Biblical. It teaches children that they are not good enough and need to be removed from us and pushed away when they are in the wrong. This is the opposite of what God wants of us. God wants us to draw near to him in times of trouble. If we are to be Christians and "Christ-like" then we should draw our children near and pray through situations.

She has a point. However, foster or adopted children have a strong tendency for emotional and behavioral issues. There are times when they need to remove themselves from situations and "reset". I also think it is important that children have time to think about their actions and assess what got them in trouble.

Children in foster care have experienced unknown previous punishments from their parents which were, most likely, negative experiences. Child intervention specialists, therapists, teachers, previous foster homes, day cares, all contributed to multiple forms of discipline. If you have a foster child, this list of people is the norm. These children learn at a young age not to know what is expected. Inconsistency is their constant.

When you have a child come to your home, set guidelines and expectations. Keep it simple and make sure they understand the consequences. Stick to the rules every time or it will not work. You are a parent, not their friend. Children want and need guidelines. Most children want approval and guidelines help them work for that approval. This is a natural approach for your child to follow. Set goals.

Biblical Reflection

Goal Seeking – Book of Nehemiah

Raising a foster/adoptive child requires perseverance, persistence, and prayerful guidance. Even though it was met with resistance, Nehemiah's goal was eventually accomplished. He had to acquire written authorization from kings, posted around the clock armed guards, and likely maintain an ongoing fire at the gate. Nehemiah had a mission he was carrying out for God. He had a goal and a team. Success didn't happen overnight. Along the way he was ridiculed and despised as people tried to sabotage their work.

Taking a child into your home is going to take more than just you. It will take the help of friends and family. Some people in your life will likely look down on you. There will be comments: *What's the matter? Can't you have your own kids?* Or, *do you even know what you are doing? They are going to have so many issues.* It will surprise you what some people will say. Surround yourself with supportive friends and family. You are doing God's work. Keep that in mind. Everyone has fallen short of the glory of God, but we are all God's children. We all need to be saved, physically and spiritually. Stay focused on God's goal. Get a team.

What goals are you going to set? How is God going to be part of that? Who is going to be on your team?

_____

_____

_____

_____

_____

_____

Prayer-

Lord, keep me focused on your goal and the ability to address negative responses to the mission You are guiding me to. Put the right people in my life who I can rely on and trust. -Amen

CHRISTMAS TIME

I TALK AT LENGTH about the calling to be foster parents and following God's will. Most of that goes together with keeping the child(ren)'s interests at heart. When it comes to Christmas, the warm fuzzy feelings start taking over and you begin picturing Christmas cards and traditions in your head. You start picking out presents and hoping you selected that perfect gift for their first Christmas at your home. You have lofty ideas that years from now they will remember when they got that cool bike, or that remote-controlled car. These aspirations are floating in the air when you plan a get-together and look forward to friends and family seeing your new family.

The sad reality is many foster kids struggle with the holidays. Memories are drummed up from past experiences once they witness families socializing. They may be wondering what their family is doing for the holiday. Who is there? Do they miss me? Do they care that I'm not there? Other thoughts could lead to remembering family arguments or trauma. When a loved one is lost near the holidays people struggle. Foster-adoptive children can have a shared experience with those who have lost people during the holidays.

These children are in a different home, different group of friends, and probably a different school system. Understanding this and surrounding them with comfort is key. Knowing this leading into the holidays can be helpful. Maybe even a conversation with your close family members beforehand could be helpful. If you see your child struggling during these holidays, be willing to put them first over your plans. This will create trust with them.

Our first Christmas with the boys was a unique experience. The first family dinner was a little crowded and loud. We saw one of our kids beginning to have anxiety about it. He was squirming around and ended up crawling under the dinner table and not moving. It was a bit awkward, especially when I knew pushing the situation would lead to a full melt-down. The situation became even more interesting when trying to tell relatives to ignore him. No parenting judgement there at all.

That evening I enjoyed staying up late putting together toys. That was something I always looked forward to doing when I was a child. One day I would be dad staying up late putting together toys for Christmas. I looked forward to being Santa.

As I was putting together the toys, I was thinking about how excited the boys would be to see them in the morning. I always loved waking to Christmas morning and storming into the family room looking at all my presents. The excitement was too much to hold back!

Christmas morning came and they started coming out of their rooms walking!!! Walked! I became nervously hesitant. They walked down the hall and saw their presents, then just looked at us. We had to tell them to go see what they got and to play. Rae and I turned to each other in question. We didn't get it. What was wrong? After discussing it we wondered if they had ever experienced this before. It made us a bit depressed thinking about it. Looking back at this years later, with more information, I believe we were correct.

Biblical Reflection

New Tradition – Matthew Chapter 1 and Luke Chapter 2
Joseph uprooted his life and followed God and Mary. He was going to quietly divorce her. He instead followed God which sparked

new tradition. He was understanding. Be understanding during the holidays.

Why do we celebrate Christmas? Some people root themselves in tradition and everything being perfect. Santa either put all the presents together and they are open under the tree, or he wrapped them all. Every family has their traditions. Your child likely had their own tradition before coming to your home. As much as you won't want to change your traditions, they won't either. Start a new one.

Establish new traditions with your children. Try to remind family members ahead of time to be understanding of what your child may experience or feel. Remember that Christ was a surprise and inconvenient upon his entry to this world. Be Joseph, the adoptive father of Christ. Adapt.

What can you do to help your child through the holidays? What is something you can do to help distract your child from chaotic moments? What are some things you could see your child struggle with, in your current traditions?

Don't wait for issues to present themselves. Try to prepare for them and have a plan.

_____

_____

_____

_____

_____

_____

Prayer-

Dear God, help me to be willing to put my personal traditions and desires aside for my child's. Help me to keep an eye

on the bigger picture and build a stronger relationship with my child. Help me to do what is necessary to make them comfortable and at ease during tough seasons and holidays.
-Amen

Parenting Other Parent's Children

ONE OF OUR KIDS had us at a crossroads. From the time he broke down in Walmart we had a different kid. Meltdowns and explosions were now a regular occurrence. Routine calls from school were the norm. We sought advice from counselors and therapists. It was here I learned how foolish professional advice can be. He would get in trouble at school for language or lying and the advice was, "Ignore it, it is only for attention.". Not only did this not settle well with me, but how is that response going to stop this behavior?

It started going through my mind; if this was my own child, what would I do? In situations like this you commonly reflect on what you experienced as a child. I would have gotten a lecture on proper Christian behavior, a swat on the butt, an early bedtime, and required to apologize to the teacher.

In reflection on this, I realized our discipline was going to need to be tailored. Rae and I were still teaching our children who Christ was and legally, a swat was not allowed. Even if I could have spanked our child, I did not know if we should. We had no idea what he had experienced in the past. The wrong approach could make this situation worse.

After several months behaviors escalated and at times got physical. I talked to Rae, and she agreed to scrap all the playbooks counselors had given us. It was illogical. I used to speed and do donuts in the street, but I never got out of a ticket because a cop knew I was doing it for attention. An effective approach would be to figure out why our child was not listening to authority figures and to address their desire for negative attention over positive attention. Answering that question was going to help. Ignoring it would not.

To start curbing his behavior and bring a semblance of sanity back to our house we had to figure this out. What did we know? Why did we think this behavior was occurring? What knowledge did we have about his past? This child was rewarded for bad behavior and taught to cuss by the father. The mother never spent any time with her children after they were two years old. She only liked babies.

This sibling group was taken from their home due to severe neglect. This is all we knew. It wasn't hard to figure out why we were having problems. The question was how to flush this attitude out of his system, especially amongst weekly visits seeing the mother?

We sat our kiddo down and laid out our rules and why they existed. Then we explained boldly what his actions were doing and why he was likely doing it. We explained that his father was in jail for doing some horrible things and we reasoned with him a bit that he wasn't making good decisions and should follow role models who were not in trouble. We explained that it was not wrong to like his father, but he should not do some of the things his father did. There are consequences beyond this house and our discipline for those actions.

This was honestly a last-ditch effort for Rae and me. He was becoming violent, kicking us both, and hurting his brother at times. If the foster agency knew what he was doing during this time it could have resulted in him being separated from his brother.

We pulled all the toys out of the room until good behavior was displayed. At this point both boys were feeding off each other. One by one they earned toys back with good behavior. It took a while for them to even want to earn toys back. They grew up without them. It was pathetic to look in their bedroom. There was nothing except for a bunk bed, which seemed harsh. We explained clearly that this was the result of breaking and throwing toys when they were mad, so everything was gone.

The underlying cause of this behavior at its core was grief of not being with their whole birth family and we were being tested. They wanted to know if we were sticking around. In one meltdown I held one of our boys while he was kicking and screaming. I told him, "You aren't going anywhere. You aren't going to run us off. You are staying in this house." After a couple more months, meltdowns cut back quite a bit.

Time passed by and we learned ways to manage. Certain things set them both off. Like, a specific way we drove to school. It took a long time to figure out why one of them would just stop talking in the car. He would get a sullen attitude right after laughing. Rae finally put it together one day. Visits with their mom were in a building we passed on the way to school. After watching closely one day, I noticed they would turn and look at the building then sink their head and not talk. The scenic route was bumpy and about ten minutes longer but helping him have a good start to the day began changing things.

Soon we started to see the signs they would exhibit before a breakdown. At this point it was not too late to preempt negative behaviors. It required us knuckling under and making some changes when approaching them. If they curled up in a corner, pushing them to say what was wrong only made things worse. I began just saying, "I'm here if you want to talk". If they were not in a full meltdown or hurting someone, we did not push it.

Soon after we cleared a few hurdles on behavior, we were approached by our foster agency. They were planning for termination of parental rights. This meant they were looking towards us adopting our kiddos. We knew this was what we were supposed to do and had prayed hard about it. However, during this time we found out our kids' sisters did not have a foster family that was making this commitment. This meant they could go to a family that would not keep in touch, or they could even be adopted out of state.

Rae and I went on a date a couple of days later. Like most husband/wife dates we were ecstatic to be "child free". So, on our date naturally we talked about our kids. We began trying to analyze our kids' behavior and predict what would happen if they didn't see their sisters again. It brought up the question; if they were with their sisters would behaviors improve? Or, would two additional children with trauma be a disservice to the progress we could make if we remained focused on our two?

From the time we taught our boys to pray, our oldest would pray for his sisters to be safe. Then he would always ask us where they were. This prompted me. I truly believed if they were all in the same house they would behave better and feel more comfortable. Rae thought I was crazy. I knew if we did it our house would be like a sardine can and we would have to move at some point. A lot of prayer was involved in acting on this thought. If we were wrong, splitting them up again would be intolerable. There would be no going back from this.

We decided to invite the sisters over to play with their brothers. It was a bit chaotic, but a lot of fun. The girls were well behaved and seemed excited. The look in the eyes of our boys was pure joy! We knew this could be a step in the right direction if done right. The next couple of days we began trying to decide what to do. I wanted to do some construction in our basement and add a couple of rooms. The only other option was finishing our upstairs. Six people were going to make our 1,000 sq ft home crammed.

We talked with our foster agency and were told if we added a room the girls could come live with us. For us to build a room in our basement we needed approval from the fire marshal, who promptly said we needed a second form of egress. Scratch that! Then we started talking about the upstairs and the agency said because all our children were under age eight, we needed to all be on the same floor. The sarcastic inner self had to hold back some words. This would have been pertinent information before these discussions and having the fire marshal over.

The only other dreaded option was the large front porch. Yes, we ended up finishing that in. This was done on the condition it was Rae's and my bedroom. The first night we stayed in that room I remember thinking how ridiculous it was. However, Rae liked the brick wall and was laughing. It helped to have a glass half full perspective during my feelings of disbelief in the moment. As I lay there, I felt like I worked my tail off 60-80 hours a week to provide a better way of life and kicked myself out to the dog's old bedroom as a reward for my efforts. I just had to find comfort in the knowledge we were doing God's will.

A couple of days later the girls arrived at our house. That night our oldest son prayed and said, "Thank you God for having our sisters live with us now." I cried a bit and knew we were doing the right thing.

Biblical Reflection

Praise in the Storm

1 Thessalonians 5:16-18, "Rejoice always, pray continually, give thanks in all circumstances; for this is God's will for you in Christ Jesus".

Sometimes just on the other side of suffering and heartache is God's glory. If it were not for the suffering of one child, we may not have disrupted our lives to help the family unit. We saw the hurt of one child and that opened Rae and I up to the hurt this group of siblings was feeling. Addressing that hurt answered a little boy's prayer.

God is in control. When we are blinded by the rain, engulfed by the storm, He sees the sunshine just on the other side. The only way we can get through the storms of our life is by reaching out and grabbing Christ's hand, so we don't get lost.

What are the storms of your life? Is there anything blinding you from God's will? Is there something preventing you from fully trusting in God?

_____

_____

_____

_____

_____

_____

Prayer-

Lord, help me to seek you even when all seems lost. Give me the perseverance to push past the struggles this world throws my way. Help me to stay focused on your will for my life and know you are in control. -Amen

THE GIRLS

I WOULD BE LYING if I said going from the responsibility of having a wife and two dogs to adding four children in a year was not overwhelming. Our house was not quiet anymore. It was fun and nuts all at the same time. We had different struggles with the girls in the mix. Overall, they were well behaved, but our oldest girl was trying to be the mom. We could tell she had some feelings that needed venting. If any of her siblings started airing any dirty laundry about their birth home, they received a death glare. It was obvious she had loyalty to her birth mom. This was understandable and sad all at the same time.

We eventually had to be bold with her and push her to just be a kid. We have a mom in the house now and she didn't need to bear that burden anymore. She was the toughest one to get to open up to us. It was like she took the role of holding the entire family together.

Her sister had a language problem and did not enjoy the idea of authority when she came to our house. For the most part, she was well behaved, and these run-ins were few and far between. We had a come to the Lord conversation about cursing and name calling. I think she honestly became too scared to try it again.

Once again, we addressed the underlying issue of name calling, profanity, and respect. This led to a new rule in our house. Adults were going to be addressed as Sir and Ma'am. I was raised in a family that supported this level of respect. Culture seems to have dropped this from being a prominent part of manners. It helped curb disrespect in our house by establishing who was in charge before disrespect exited their mouths.

It is easy to travel down the roads of do's and don'ts with children. Our society has evolved into a state of mind where we are so busy that we neglect basic respect. We communicate through email, we message things we would never say in person, etc. It is easy to fall into this mindset when raising a child as well.

We were thrown into the deep end of the metaphorical pool with four children who all did appalling things right off the bat. I was floored on more than one occasion with the thought going through my mind, "I don't think I could even call my parents to get their ideas on how to handle this, because I never would have even thought of doing that!" After one child kicked Rae and another called her an "F-ing B". I realized we skipped the respect chapter in our invisible handbook. We needed to start at square one.

They were never taught respect. They didn't even know what it meant. The first step in teaching respect is acknowledging it every time you speak to an adult. Yes Ma'am, No Ma'am, Yes Sir, No Sir. It became mandatory at our house anytime they talked to us. We called their teachers to make sure they were using it at school as well.

Ma'am became one of our youngest son's first words. I did not have much of a problem with the kids showing me respect. I was the adult male. They were taught at their biological home that women did not matter, and no respect was needed for them. After troubleshooting the cause of some of our issues, it was clear verbal manners were going to be pushed with our children.

There is a lesson in this story. There is a time and place for everything. Ignoring behaviors will not fix them. Teaching do's and don'ts leads to raising a child with no foundation. Why should we do this? Why shouldn't we do this? I believe the foundation of who we are is in direct correlation to our spiritual health. If I ignore my child's spirit it won't heal itself. Our kids pray every night before bed, and we make sure to do devotions and use the Bible to help us parent. This instills purpose in why we are doing what we are doing and paves a way for our children to follow.

Biblical Reflection

Respect – Matthew 7:12 *"So in everything, do to others what you would have them do to you, for this sums up the Law and the Prophets"*.

James 3:5-6 *"Likewise, the tongue is a small part of the body, but it makes great boasts. Consider what a great forest is set on fire by a small spark. The tongue also is a fire, a world of evil among the parts of the body. It corrupts the whole body, sets the whole course of one's life on fire, and is itself set on fire by hell."*

It is easy to dismiss the gravity of these verses. Society tells us to get even when someone treats us wrong. Peer pressure tells us to just ignore foul language. As parents we need to equip our children to be God's voice in a society that rejects it.

The degradation of society is a reason many young couples are neglecting to have children. God has called us time and time again to be fruitful and multiply the earth. We have a mentality of removing potentially ethical children from being born by quality people, out of fear. If you are removing good from God's world evil will be increasingly prominent in years to come.

Equip your children. Teach them to show God's love. Don't ignore disrespect and foul language. Lead by example. Most of the language and attitude a child learns comes from home.

Are you prepared to address these issues? Are there areas of your life that may need straightened up to lead by example?

_____

_____

_____

_____

_____

_____

Prayer-

Heavenly Father, help me be the example my child needs. Help them see you in my actions. Curb my language and attitude to be glorifying to you. -Amen

HOME INVASION

AS FREE SPIRITED AS Rae and I once were the biggest struggle we experienced were agencies in our house **ALL THE TIME**. Once the girls came to live with us privacy went out the window. Our youngest had a play therapist and a speech therapist. All four kids had an intensive placement stabilization therapist, due to being moved so many times. All three of these appointments were weekly at our home. Then we had two CASA workers, one for the girls and one for the boys. CASA is an agency that advocates for the child's best interest before the court. The social worker stopped by routinely, as well as the transporter who drove the kids to their weekly visits with their mother. This schedule was horrible. Once or twice a month we had six different people in our house during a given week. If someone neglected to get their visit in, the world seemed to stop spinning.

I vividly remember driving home sick from a business trip off the heels of working 80 hours that week to a child also sick at home. One of these workers called demanding to see the kids on Sunday. Sunday!!! The fact that some of us were sick and throwing up meant nothing. They still demanded to see us. They were incredibly rude and said they had to get their paperwork together. It was the end of the month and they had procrastinated.

I will refrain from going into detail about what was said by either of us. These are times you must stand up for your family time as well as your sanity. Poor preparation on their part does not constitute an emergency on your part. The tricky thing is you do not want a bad review of your parenting skills from a person who presents before the judge. Family comes first and there are times when you need to put your foot down.

Most workers with these agencies are underpaid, overworked, and lack a fear of losing their jobs. There are side-effects of this atmosphere. Most of the people we worked with were great, but it is important to establish boundaries. You are trying to create a warm, stable environment for children who have known only chaos. Try to avoid additional chaos.

I do not know how Rae kept up with the kids' schedules. At this point she had them in sports and every one of our kids had an IEP (Individualized Education Plan) for school. They were all delayed in school due to neglect and switching schools, as well as homes, often. Getting homework done with all of them was a chore. Having people in our house every evening began to physically drain us.

Mondays and Tuesdays were the days to expect someone at our house in the evening. Wednesday was church, and Thursdays I had band practice, Fridays we tried to have family time, but sometimes there were people at our house. It was complete chaos, and we were running two businesses. Someone would leave then someone else showed up. I felt like our house was a medical clinic.

Eventually, we had to weed out which services were necessary and which ones we could let go. We paired up with CASA to have visits at the same time, typically at a park to remove chaos from our home. Some of the therapy sessions were cut out and we started advocating for services available through the school system. Again, chaos removed from the home. Little things here and there started to help.

Developing a relationship with your child is important. It seems that adults gravitate to other adults when dealing with what is best for their child. TALK TO YOUR CHILD! The people in family services may have thirty children they juggle paperwork for. It is a mess. They constantly have court dates and get calls at all hours to find a home for a child. Meanwhile, they are keeping medical history and school paperwork organized. Add to that, anytime one of their foster kids goes to the doctor they are made aware of it.

Think about all of this and multiply it by the number of people who work with your child. Who do you want to know your child better? Develop a relationship with your kid(s) and take time to talk with them. Make sure they feel comfortable approaching you. Sometimes the people working with them may not be the people you want working with them. If a worker provokes your child, make sure you are aware of it.

We had a person driving the kids to their visits with their mom who violated so many rules it made Rae and I furious. She would talk down to just one of our kids. She left the mom alone with the kids, which is a violation for obvious reasons. Most infuriating was her inaccurate reports of what happened in visits because she felt sorry for the birth mom. We were unaware of most of these things. Our youngest son was potty trained for two months. Then suddenly he was not. We had no clue what caused this and then one of our kids told us that at the visits the mom had started taking him to the bathroom by himself. Shortly after this, our other son began having bathroom problems.

We eventually partnered with one of the therapists to observe visits to have other eyes on what was going on. The boat began to rock quickly, and issues aired themselves out. It is important to think outside the box, so children are protected and do not fall through the cracks.

Biblical Reflection

Rest

*Genesis 2:2 "By the seventh day God had finished the work
he had been doing; so on the seventh day he rested from all
his work."*

I have an uncle who is a retired heavy equipment mechanic. His
job was to work along job sites and keep the equipment functioning.
In the wintertime up in the mountains, the diesel tanks would get so
cold that even while the machines were running the diesel fuel would
get cold enough that it would turn "gel-like"; and the engines would
stop. Because of the demand to get projects done they had people
next to the machines with torches regularly heating up the tanks, trying to keep the machines from shutting down because the process of
warming up the diesel tanks took too long. Even then, sometimes the
engines would stop.

Can you relate to this mentality? When our bodies and our minds
want a break, we are pushed to keep going. We live in a society de-
signed to consume any dead time available. You must know your limits. What is best for your family? God established a day of rest from
the start. He knew we needed it. With an increasingly secular society,
that mentality has all but died out over the last 50 years. In the past
three years mental health disorders have increased by 25% (Forbes,
2023). As a parent, it is your job to know your limits and do what is
best for the health of your family. Build in rest time. Take this time
to have conversations with your children and check-in. Rest and recharge. If you neglect rest, your life will be in unrest.

What kind of atmosphere are you going to provide for your family? What are some ways you can ensure family time? Is your life too busy? What can you do to change that?

_____

_____

_____

_____

_____

_____

_____

Prayer-

Lord, make me aware of the mental needs of my family. Help us to reach out to You for spiritual peace in our lives. Give us the strength to say no when necessary and to keep rest a part of our lives. -Amen

TRUCK STORY

RAE HAD A SEASONAL business with three locations. I would open one location and close two with the kids and she closed the last one each day. These businesses were outside. I would roll the windows down in the truck and walk about twenty feet, close, and five minutes later I was back in the truck to the other location.

One day I came back to a horrible stench which filled the air after turning on the air conditioner. I looked at that back seat and it was wet. I asked, "Did someone wet their pants?" Much to my dismay I guessed the correct assailant. "Why didn't you ask to use the restroom?" All I got was a shoulder shrug. I was frustrated but controlled myself. Later I cleaned it up the best I could, but it still smelled, and it was the heat of summer.

The same day one week later we were closing the same spot and location again. He asks this time, "Can I use the bathroom?" I was currently in the middle of pushing the cart away and I said, "Give me one second bud". Tough situation... is he going to do it again? I can't leave what I'm doing though. Plus, he is a "runner", so I never trust him to go by himself.

Two minutes later I got back to the truck and started to drive off. I then turned around and said, "Wait didn't you have to use the restroom?" I looked around and his sister was wet. The truck was wet. The smell may as well have slapped me in the face. I looked up front and his other sister had a couple spots in her hair that were wet. I lost it and yelled, "WHAT HAPPENED?" Our youngest daughter said, "He pulled down his pants and started peeing everywhere!" I looked at him and he said sheepishly, "I had to go". Trying to filter my thoughts I said, "You used the restroom at our house before leaving. It is a 10-minute drive here. I took 5-minutes and you just had to go so bad you decided to flip out your privates in front of your sisters and brother, pee on them, then see if you could arch it over the front seat and get your sister there too?" All I got was shoulder shrugs.

This story is one of the toughest I have had to deal with. He told me he had to go. Most of the time he doesn't have to go and is just bored. I couldn't leave what I was doing. Still, peeing on people is inappropriate and completely wrong. I started to analyze the events and landed a thousand directions as to why this happened.

- He was mad because he asked, and I said I was busy and to wait a second. So, it ended up in an outlandish retaliation.
- He was seeing what I would do because last week I said, "It better not happen again. In the future ask to use the restroom". He wanted to see the worst punishment I had and was testing me. This one made me nervous.
- Both times this happened were on days he had visits with his mother. Subconsciously he was trying to show himself loyal to his birth parents.
- All the above.

How do you discipline this? He asked to use the restroom, but he was still wrong in the manner he peed. Had he just peed his pants I obviously would have him start using the restroom as soon as we got there and not just at the house.

- I stayed calm after my initial outburst and took the kids to our music store (closest location to clean up)

- I sat him in a corner while I settled down and cleaned the kids up.
- I had a stern conversation about the fact I understood he had to use the restroom (validate his position) but pulling down your pants in front of your brother and sisters is not acceptable. And peeing on them is in no way right.
- Shampoo cost for my truck seats was $40. He owed me four hours of cleaning time. Wherever possible tie your form of discipline directly to what they did. His four hours were spent at that business cleaning up. There was no way he was going to get the smell out of my truck himself. Instead, he had to clean something else.

It may have seemed wrong that I disciplined him when he said he had to go. However, there was a strong push on his part to test the level of boundaries. If this was not addressed immediately and strictly what would stop him from doing it again? Kids will always push the gray area. Especially children who have been able to push boundaries with other authority figures in the past.

Know your child and try to get an insight into their history. At times it is easy to get frustrated with your child, but they are a product of their history. You can be the impact for their future.

Biblical Reflection

Patience

Judges 6:36-40 *"Gideon said to God, "If you will save Israel by my hand as you have promised— look, I will place a wool fleece on the threshing floor. If there is dew only on the fleece and all the ground is dry, then I will know that you will save Israel by my hand, as you said." And that is what happened. Gideon rose early the next day; he squeezed the fleece and wrung out the dew—a bowlful of water.*

Then Gideon said to God, "Do not be angry with me. Let me make just one more request. Allow me one more test with the fleece, but this time make the fleece dry and let the ground be covered with dew." That night God did so. Only the fleece was dry; all the ground was covered with dew."

We have all had moments where we wanted to be like Gideon. We like to get clear answers from God and test him. When God speaks, we like to verify what we heard because it seems so ridiculous. We are confronted with weighing our knowledge of God's grace and will against our human experiences. This is a much smaller image against God's bird's eye view.

Imagine you are a child who has been bounced around, traumatized, and never truly had someone they could rely on to take care of them. You come into their lives and say that you will do what no one has ever done. You will be that support that they cannot comprehend. You will do something they have never experienced. Just as God indulged Gideon with grace and understanding, you will need to as well. If you are the voice of God's will and perseverance in your child's mind, they will test you. Have a Christ-like response to your tests. Have patience.

Put yourself in your child's shoes. Can you gain insight into behaviors you have seen, or may see in the future? Do you see the importance of grace? Get into a mindset that is beyond the simple black and white during these tests. God did.

_____

_____

_____

-Prayer

Heavenly Father, give me strength and patience during my child's testing. Help me display just a portion of the grace you have shown me. Just as my child is trying me, and will in the future, help them see Jesus' grace shone through me.
-Amen

CHRIST LED DISCIPLINE

WHEN A CHILD MISBEHAVES, find a discipline that fits the crime. I have spoken about assigning costs and figuring out how much a given incident costs to have your assailant work off the mishap. This means they must work for how many hours wages it took us to pay for it. This can be frustrating when you realize that you personally worked three or four hours to pay for something that was broken on purpose. It is important to view these times as teachable moments and not to exacerbate the situation by exploding your feelings out to them, prompting further destruction of property, and your relationship.

If you adopt a sibling group, chaos tends to feed on itself. Calculating the financial destruction is enough to send someone over the edge. If you follow my advice on assigning work to pay off property abuse, you will eventually be confronted with the fact that your child did not actually make you money to replace the item you may very much need. The math is extremely frustrating when figuring financial damages.

Did you know that a kitchen cabinet can't hold a 10-year-old during hide and seek? Or, that a ceiling fan blade can't hold an 8-year-old? If you overreact filled with anger during these times, you have further increased the barrier you are trying to overcome with trust. This does not mean that you underreact.

Be aware that foster adoptive children tend to have strong feelings of rejection. If you react in a rejecting manner towards them, you fall into a category where you are associated with those who rejected them in the past. You may have valid reasons for losing your patience. In their eyes, your reaction to their behavior is what is being observed. Again, put yourself in their shoes.

Your reaction needs to be viewed through an evangelical lens as well. You are likely introducing them to Christ and religion in your home. What impression are you giving them? Is it forgiveness? Is it love? It is better to go for a walk or drive and come back with a clear head than to show "understandable", yet potentially relationship hindering reactions in a sensitive situation. You are being tested and you must pass the test.

I have overreacted at times, lost my patience, and probably cost six months of progress more than once. It is important to own up to your mistakes. Apologize to your child for your outburst and "negative" behavior, even if they stole a couple hundred dollars from your wallet with no hope of explaining how they obtained it.

Some of the most effective progress Rae and I have made was by setting a child on a couch, looking right at them for a while, and saying nothing when we are upset. This will tell you whether they care about what they did. That will help determine the discipline. It will hopefully help you address the situation in a more effective manner. If you see remorse in their eyes, it will help you cool down too.

Biblical Reflection

Direction

Proverbs 22:6 Start children off on the way they should go, and even when they are old they will not turn from it.

If you gain insight into your child's biological family, you will likely have the conversation of "nurture versus nature". You will notice ticks, habits, and eccentricities that were not learned from you or your spouse. You will determine that it was "nature", it is their DNA that put that "manner" into your child.

You can do everything in your power to raise a child in the way they should go and "nurture" them in a proper lifestyle that is glorifying for God, but they may eventually reject your teaching. In those situations, how do we rationalize scriptures like Proverbs 22:6?

The Book of Proverbs is a guideline for life. It is not a promise. One example of this is seen in Noah's family. God saw Noah as good and rebuilt the earth around this one family. Noah's son Ham turned, and his son Cannan was cursed; leading way to the Canaanites that would one day be wiped out by the Israelites.

The best chance any parent can have at seeing this scripture come to fruition is through physical discipline and spiritual transformation. Bring the love of Christ into your discipline and raising of your child. Make sure their understanding of the rules in your home is not based on you, but on God.

Explain why it is important. Why do your rules exist? Do your rules exist to glorify God? Do your forms of discipline glorify God? Will they lead your child toward God, or away?

_____

_____

_____

_____

_____

_____

Prayer –

Lord, help me to create a foundation in our home that is going to glorify you and the future of my child. Help me to show your grace and mercy in discipline and raising of them. I know the gravity of my time in their life. Help me to make the most of it so they will know you in their life. -Amen

Advocating for your
Children

NOT LONG AFTER THE girls came to live with us the birth mom's attorney started to push for visits to be held at her home rather than at a Child and Family Service's building. This was tough. Most of the time this is a step toward the children going back home. The thought of losing our children was intolerable. At this point we established strong relationships with them. They had told us stories about what it was like before foster care. It was impossible for us to imagine them going back to that kind of environment.

In recent years I have come to struggle with divulging much of what I know about our kids' birth parent situation. It is their story to tell, not mine. To be a true Christian follower and leader you take "Christ-like" behavior through all aspects of life. So, when you find yourself confronted with a situation like this you struggle to rationalize how you should pray. You should never want to see a family ripped apart. However, you do not want to see children go back to a bad situation.

To give context to the struggle Rae and I had praying through this situation I will share a small picture of our kids' story. A minimum of three large families lived in a small house where the older kids would all sleep on the couch together. If they were hungry, they would see if food was in the garbage can. Our oldest would talk about hearing her youngest sibling cry at night because he was hungry. They also witnessed far too much of their parents' promiscuous lifestyle.

These were tough conversations to have when our children began talking to us. When your child begins unloading the weight on them, just let them talk. Avoid putting your child in a mindset that could prompt them choosing the side of foster parents over birth parents. Let them expel their feelings freely. This will allow you to gain insight into their character and emotional health.

Ask them non-condemning questions that keep them talking (i.e., How did that make you feel? What are your thoughts on that?). The more they divulge to you the more trust they build. Knowing more about their past and mindset allows you to better handle guiding their future.

View these situations as teachable moments for yourself and not them. If they are sharing something traumatic about their past, avoid navigating into what should have gone right, what was wrong, or what they could have done better... unless they genuinely ask your advice. They are trying to trust you. If you respond incorrectly in their eyes, then they will likely feel ashamed or inadequate. Just listen, be an ear, show compassion. Be "Christ-like".

Signing up for foster parenting is tough when you are wanting to adopt. Your mindset is immediately set to long term attachments with your children. As a Christian you know in your heart if the situation was different you would pray for the family to find strength and seek Jesus out. You would pray that they get their life in order. However, if they do this you could lose your children. It is a double-edged sword in your mind. It is a struggle that has you feeling like a bad Christian. God has a plan for you and the children. They may be separate plans, but if you have the strength to seek God through the process then he will be with you on the other side.

My wife and I knew this would be a struggle when starting on this path. We were advised if we wanted to adopt, other agencies would be better. The other side to this was knowledge that most children did not go back to biological homes permanently in Illinois. It is very hard to have a child removed from biological parents in this foster system. If it was bad enough to have children removed, then the biological parents were likely so lost that they did not take the necessary steps to get their children back.

The prayer that stuck in my mind through our struggle was, "Dear Jesus, give me strength and wisdom through this. Help me follow Your lead in my life. I pray Your will be done in this situation and help the parents see what is happening to their family. They need You in their lives and need You to help them stop the cycle of brokenness." We must do everything in our power to ensure the generational sin ends with our spiritual guidance.

I tried not to take sides in these prayers. When you search your heart, do you really have it in yourself to pray they lose legal rights to their children? Do you have it in your heart to pray they get them back when you know they are possibly at the lowest spot in their life? It is easy to put yourself down for your feelings in this position, but they are natural feelings. These are also questions to address before committing to foster care. However, if you commit to it that is why you have your questions ready (i.e., Are they legal risk? Where are the parents? Do they have visits? Where are those visits?)

When our children were placed with us the father was in jail and the mother had no car or job. It was unlikely the kids would go home. Our kids had weekly visits with their mother. They were supervised and only one hour. The children were pulled from their home due to severe neglect. There was no evidence of drugs, alcohol, etc. They just couldn't properly raise children.

The parents had been in the foster care system themselves and were repeating their experience with their children. This is a common foster situation, but most of the time drugs or alcoholism is involved. As foster parents, it pushed our prayer life. It was logical in my mind to believe if they were on drugs or alcohol they could go to rehab. If they lost their job and home, then they could eventually get a job and suitable place. In this situation the house was extremely overcrowded, and the children had no food to eat when a caseworker stopped by.

With this knowledge it was hard to find it in our hearts to say those impartial and loving prayers. I prayed about how to pray. If it was God's will, He could have intervened and changed that whole family. We would have lost our beautiful children, but God's mission could have still been achieved in expanding the kingdom and ending the cycle of sin. The goal behind adoption is to give a loving home to a child in need. If a mother and father find Jesus in the rubble of their lives how can a Christian stand in the way?

ILLOGICAL LOGIC

LIFE IS A CONSTANT state of unexpected occurrences. Waking up each day brings a new experience or stress. One of the most miserable stresses out there is lice. I never had it growing up, but it came to our house.

I got the call from work and Rae started freaking out a bit... as she should. I went to pick up the rest of our kids and the lice had spread to them all. The daycare had no other kids with it and the schools didn't have any issues. I didn't have it! Where did it come from? Their birth mother's house was the issue. *How do we deal with this?* Lice hatch a pattern of 7-10 days. That meant weekly visits to their mother's house would cause an entire cycle of cleaning out bedding, clothes, expensive hair wash, etc., EVERY WEEK! It would seem an open and shut case to have the birth mom clean her house, treat everything, and skip a week or two of visits, right?

The case worker said they still had to go! This seemed like the most illogical and impossible fight. Rae couldn't go back to work because the kids had to stay home. This couldn't be happening every week until the lice miraculously died on their own. Many times, the decisions of children and family services make little since. It is up to the foster parents to fight for what is right. We had a talk with the driver for the agency that transported the kids to and from visits and informed her that the kids had lice. We not so subtly questioned whether she would still drive them because she probably would not want to get lice in her car. This fixed the situation and she refused to take them.

A couple of weeks later she personally examined the house and made sure the mom also didn't have lice. From that point on we made the kids strip down and shower after their visits. We stuck the clothes straight into the washing machine.

Our kids were not too happy with having lice and went on to explain that they used to get it a lot. Our boys would get their heads shaved. Figuring out how to navigate fighting for logical reasoning is a big part of being a foster parent. Learn "not" to avoid it. Stand up for your kids! They are trapped inside a government agency. Just think about that.

A typical morning for our family now consists of getting our kids off to school and making sure they look presentable, and they have their homework done. We go to work and make money to provide for our family. It once also included dealing with agencies and a whole other family that could blindside you every day. It is important to realize during those times you are doing God's work and taking care of His child. Be that voice the child needs. You are in a tough mission field.

Biblical Reflection

Staying Calm Don't Worry

-*Proverbs 15:18"Hotheads stir up conflict, but patient people calm down strife."*

- *Philippians 4:6-7 "Do not be anxious about anything, but in every situation, by prayer and petition, with thanksgiving, present your requests to God. And the peace of God, which transcends all understanding, will guard your hearts and your minds in Christ Jesus."*

It is enticing at times to unload your frustrations and feelings on what seems illogical. Many times, the first person you see receives the brunt of your anger. This tends to gain little momentum toward rectifying a situation. Slow down and pray through the situation. Come back with a fresh look at the problem and think outside of the box.

Many people misread Philippians 4:6-7. Do not be anxious and taking worries to God is far from physically neglecting the issue. Many people stop at prayer. Taking concerns to God in prayer is seeking advice. Most concerns need to be physically addressed and not neglected. Stand up for your child in the direction and manner God calls to you.

Do you get anxiety during confrontation? Do you overanalyze situations? What is, or what could be a stumbling block for you being the voice your child needs?

_____

_____

_____

_____

_____

_____

Prayer-

Dear God, remove my worries and stresses. I know you are in control of my situation. Help me see the direction you are leading me. Give me wisdom through that path and help me to be the voice my child needs. Help the outcome be your outcome and remove my voice from being a stumbling block. Amen

Name Changer

SHORTLY BEFORE WE ADOPTED our children, we changed their names. Rae and I had discussed the possibility of doing this for safety reasons, but we were not going to push this on our children. The gravity of changing a name could go amazingly well or be a disaster. To change a child's name against their will would alienate them beyond comprehension. A name is an identity.

There is a sad joke in the "foster world" that you can spot a child in care by the black trash bags. The implication being that all their possessions are in a couple bags with no monetary value. They have nothing. Imagine taking their name as well. It is the last connection to their biological parents after parental rights are terminated.

It is for this reason changing our children's names was not our choice, but theirs. We sat our older children down and talked in depth about adopting them. We simply asked whether they would like a new name since we were all going to be a permanent family. Over the next couple of weeks, they one by one decided they wanted to do it. We clarified with them and made sure they understood what it meant to change their names. Their explanation was wanting a name from their biological parents and one from us. They chose their new names and made their old names their middle names. Once we began calling them by their new first names we saw an improvement in their behavior, which was interesting.

Rae and I questioned whether this change of behavior was due to a subconscious connection to their birth parents. They had been taught to misbehave for their foster parents, use foul language, and be defiant. Most of this bad behavior was weeded out at this point, but they seemed a bit more comfortable at home.

It was a struggle to get the school on board with this before the children were officially adopted. Finally, after questioning the difference between what we were asking and a "William" being called Bill, or a "Robert" Bob they accepted our request. Behavior improved at school as well. I believe it symbolized a fresh start in our children's minds.

During this time, we received mixed responses to changing our children's names. We received some flak from a few of the people who worked directly with them. While it can be viewed as their beliefs versus our own, I feel this subject is important to discuss.

If you look to the Bible for advice on the subject, you will find a precedent. Once God developed a personal relationship with a person, he often changed their name: Abram to Abraham, Sarai to Sarah when chosen to be good in the sight of God and chosen to be the father of many nations. Jacob to Israel, and the list goes further.

Once you answer the call of God to take a child into your home you have started a spiritual mission. That mission begins with a physical approach to raising and impacting your child. It should not end there. Jesus calls us to care for those in need, but He shared a valuable perspective with the Samaritan woman at the well in John chapter four. We can address the physical needs over and over, but if we share the Gospel message of everlasting life, we will have all that we ever need.

When you take this approach to foster and adoption then you are truly allowing God to lead your family and be a central part of ending the cycle of brokenness. He will change their hearts and intervene in a way that changes their identity, their name. Yes, their physical father has changed, but they need an introduction to their spiritual father. You are not called to simply help a child in physical need. You are called to help a child in spiritual need. This is what God has laid precedent for. Impacting God's kingdom. A name change from God means a spiritual event occurred that is going to impact the physical.

I am not advocating for renaming your child(ren). This is the perspective and path we took. Each situation is different, just make sure God is at the center of it. Every situation is different. If you are raising a 15-year-old whose parents passed away in a car crash, you probably shouldn't go down that road.

If you choose to approach this subject, do it out of love. Make them part of the process. It could build a bond in your relationship. Our experience was a best-case scenario. Yours may not be. It is important to maintain conversation with your children and be open to receiving feedback without offense.

Biblical Reflection

Identity in Christ

-Genesis 35:10 "Your name is Jacob, but you will not be called Jacob any longer. From now on your name will be Israel."

It was not until after Jacob fought with God in the dark all night that his name was changed. Our path toward God may not be pretty. It can be hard to remove ourselves from a physically persecuting world and gain a complete insight into the spiritual freedom that is invisible to us.

Just as Jacob was wounded in his fight with God, so was Paul. Many times, it is not until we are forced to slow down that we are able to focus on God's calling for our lives. When that happens, we can mentally fully dedicate our identity to Christ and leave our past in the wake.

Prayer-

Lord, I pray that my children will find their identity in You and not in the things of this world. Help me to provide a Christian atmosphere that will help bring them toward You. Help me to see when they are stumbling and need my help. Help me to never neglect the importance of what You are doing through me for them. -Amen

Get Me Out of This House!!!

I HAD A MENTAL breakdown one day. I don't know if many men have the problem of working all day, then coming home to chaos and showing a bad attitude. I have an added problem. Many of my clients are well to do. When I visit them at their homes, I see playrooms and separate parts of their homes shut off for work and from chaos. Some of them even have mansions. I would see this and drive home to a place where there was no escape from the chaos. It was a rather questionable neighborhood so I could not trust the kids to just play outside either. I would close the door to my "porch-bedroom" and try to have ten minutes of peace and quiet.

That was a joke when the neighbor boy would relentlessly knock on our front door/bedroom, or the foul-mouthed neighbor would curse at his lawn mower that just needed to be taken to the scrap yard. Part of me wanted to help him. The other part wanted to run the mower over with my truck. These frustrations were flooding my head. The only peace and quiet I ever received seemed to be in the bathroom. However, the kids' bedrooms were right next to it. Inevitably, someone would scream.

I concluded my only recourse for solitude was to be had by waking up early. I decided to get up an extra hour early. Maybe I could reenact the old routine I had before children. I could go on a quick run, take a quiet shower, grab a bowl of cereal, and sit on the couch to watch a little TV before chaos started.

As soon as I got in the shower there was a knock at the door. I wanted to cry. **"Yes?"** "Can I use the restroom?" **"Yes, then go right back to bed."** Another knock **"YEeEes?"** "Can I get my toothbrush?" **"Why are you up? It's early!"** The first child left, and Rae came in. "Why are you up so early?" **"At this point, I really don't know."** The girls then came in to use the restroom and get a glass of water. Then one of our large dogs ran in knocking someone into the wall. Then I heard our son ask, "What's for breakfast?"

Keep in mind this bathroom was about 5 feet by 6 feet. One person in the shower, one on the toilet, one at the sink, one brushing their hair, a dog, and a yelling child from the outside. I was the only guy in the room! Trying to take a shower! I just screamed!!! "I make decent money! You make decent money! We are obviously adopting these kids! Why the heck is this house not already for sale! We live on the front porch like we're broke! I'm done, this is stupid! I can't even get privacy at 6:00 am!!!" I felt bad about the level of my explosion, especially in front of the kids. Rae just laughed and said, "About time!" We had a for sale sign in the yard by the weekend.

As luck would have it, we struggled to sell our house. A two-bedroom house can be a hard sell even without six people and two large dogs in the mix. We left it for sale and eventually took it off the market when our summer business started back up. The last thing we wanted to do was move during 70 to 80-hour work weeks.

After about six months, we were losing patience with the state and the length of time the adoption was taking. Our adoption worker still did not have paperwork done. After repeated appointments with no shows from her we were peaked with stress. We could not sell our house and there seemed to be no end in sight.

Journal Entry- *The most stressful point of my life*

At 3:00 am it is obvious sleep will evade me. I have had a hard time trying to get a full night's rest. Outsiders may look upon me and think I have it together. Rae and I have prayed for God to bless us with children, and we got our prayer answered, right? We have successful businesses and four beautiful kids! What a perfect family!

I have personally had stress through the roof lately. Business has been stressful though God is telling me I am doing things correctly, which is even more stressful. Though I thought it impossible, it seems our house situation has added even more stress. I was going to do what all men do when they have been blessed with as many children as they would like. The only snag with that was our adoption took about six months longer that it should have, and God said why not one more. The day I found out my wife was pregnant was not an ideal scene from a romantic comedy movie.

I came home from work to grab a quick lunch on a Saturday. I was backed up at work finishing an amplifier build for a trip to Nashville and it had me stressed out quite a bit. Anything that could go wrong was, and the amp was for a big artist. I was a little on edge. When I got home, I could tell Rae was frazzled. There was a bit less patience on her face with our kids and she gave me a look. To be honest I wasn't sure what was wrong. The kids ran inside, and she started crying and said she was pregnant.

I have seen enough movies to know that there is only one thing the husband can say that would be the correct response. "It will be ok! Don't worry about it. This wasn't planned but it's great!" I also questioned internally whether it would truly happen this time for us. I went back to work and have yet to know how I completed that amp.

I felt like a liar to my wife. I told her what I believed to be a bold-faced lie. I was 29 years old, and my wife was 26. Less than a year earlier we had purchased our third business, the family music store. I was already scheduling anxiety into my daily routine. It immediately hit me that our house had been on the market for close to a year and not sold. How were we supposed to buy another house? Our car wouldn't fit seven of us. Financially, how can we afford to buy another house, a car, pay for a pregnancy, and front the fabulous expenses that are babies and diapers? I told myself "Trust God and don't worry".

Journal entry-4 months later

I truly am excited about our baby coming, with a bit of nerves added in. I must bring out the feelings I have had through this process from a father's perspective.

To me a good father has an innate desire to provide for his family. I need to be the strong backbone of the family. If I let my family know that I about puked coming up with the money for our second home we now live in, what good would it do?

It was only by the grace of God we came up with the down payment. They don't need to know the very recent stress I have had juggling vehicles. During this time my dad has been gone from work due to open-heart surgery and I needed to hire an extra full-time employee as well. I am not one to discuss personal finances in general, but after having a few anxiety-attacks I have learned to control my breathing and the importance of not letting things bottle up.

Every time someone says, "You have three businesses, two homes, you're adopting four kids with one on the way? Man, you have your hands full!" I must seriously focus not to go into another attack. Can I handle it? I can! God helps me! My attacks will go away when things settle down.

My anxiety started when I knew the things I needed to do and began doing them without thinking twice about it. I don't make quick decisions. My wife may believe I do, but if I buy something, I have thought about it for a couple weeks at least. I simply trusted God and He got me to where I am. I followed Him through doors that opened. The old house will be rented out soon. We have a beautiful new home and have a family vehicle now. I feel like my stress and anxiety is due to God driving the vehicle of life for me and I am just in the passenger's seat asking, "Where are we going? I must know! How are You going to handle this? What are You doing?"

My anxiety-attacks make me feel like the Israelites wandering in the desert. "Moses because there were no graves in Egypt, have you taken us to die in the wilderness?" (Exodus 14:11). It makes me feel like a poor Christian at times. My human traits are saying, "I detest debt. I do, and I have come so close to being debt free more than once. What is coming next God?" The truth is God gave me success in business and it is His business anyway! If He calls me to bring A LOT of wonderful children into our home, then why question the method He does it or the reason? A foolish man knows God's will and goes his own way.

Getting four children in our small 1000 sq ft home wasn't as earth-shattering for me as one would think. My wife and I had to pray hard because we knew if they came to our home, we would be adopting them. We knew it in our hearts. That was our need for prayer. The past six months my prayer has been for trust. "God, please help me trust You. You have a plan, and I don't know it. Please give me wisdom, strength, and help me make the right decisions. Please open and close the right doors." It is a simple prayer. When you are stressed in the middle of the day and following through with what God has called you to do, whisper that prayer and you will know you are not alone.

TRUST

OUR DESIRE TO MOVE for comfort transitioned into a necessity. Our house was busting at the seams. Our foster agency would not allow us to expand our house by finishing the basement, nor the upstairs. Our children were of the age that most of them were required to have bedrooms of the same level as us. Due to this, a baby on the way only made things worse.

We were simply months from adoption going through and we did not want to rattle cages by opening our mouths that we were pregnant. If the agency and adoption worker found out, we would have to be back to square one with a home study. "How many people live in the home?" "How many children?" The reality of the matter is that the adoption worker was close to a year behind on her paperwork as it was, and the adoption should have already taken place. We decided the best thing we could do was purchase a larger house that would accommodate our family and if we got caught there was no doubt there was enough space. They would likely let us fly without new paperwork.

This was tricky. If we purchased a new home this would require us to let the foster agency know we moved and to be approved for a different home, but we did not want the adoption agency to know. We also did not want the adoption worker to see Rae, who was now showing that she was pregnant. We faxed, emailed, and mailed several documents in lieu of a face-to-face meeting.

This whole situation sounds deceitful on our part, but the reality is that our kids at this point had been in foster care for over four years. This adoption worker had promised that the adoption would be completed six months to a year prior to this point. The question is, how long do you prolong making changes in your life based on the pace of a government agency? We were completely truthful with our original paperwork, but things changed in a year and a half from when that was completed.

The key was to complete this adoption before the baby was born, otherwise we were indeed going to be in trouble legally with the paperwork. No child was born yet so we had not lied about the number of people living in our home. For our own frustrations and not getting in trouble we needed to get the ball rolling on this adoption. We had spoken with the adoption supervisor to no avail, and even found out the supervisor's boss was a relative to our adoption worker. We concluded at this point the adoption worker was prolonging our case because we had submitted a formal complaint and she knew a family member would not fire her.

We reached out to several people for advice and found someone with close contacts to a senator. We explained to him the issues we had with our adoption worker, and he said he would make a call. Within a couple of weeks, we had an adoption date set. Rae and I calculated, and she would be pushing seven months pregnant the day of adoption. Just in the nick of time.

It was extraordinarily stressful navigating the events leading to our adoption. With the urgency to move before the agencies knew Rae was pregnant it was a tight budget. We picked a house that was perfect for our family, but we were forced to buy it without selling our current home. This meant us coming up with a down payment for a more expensive home, committing to a larger mortgage, as well as the existing mortgage on our current home.

As I said earlier, I had also hired an extra full-time person at our family music store because my dad was recovering from open-heart surgery. I felt like the walls were closing in from all areas financially. Rae kept asking me, "How are we going to make this work?" I just told her, "God was going to provide". I just knew God was going to handle the situation. I didn't know how, but He would.

I put everything I did not need up for sale online. I sold my guitar collection at my music store and came up with all but $1,500 for the down payment. It was one week until closing and we were still short $1,500 and I was feeling the pressure. Rae and I were concerned about where the money was going to come from.

Out of nowhere I got a message from someone about a vehicle I had listed for sale almost six months earlier. I honestly forgot that it was still listed... for exactly $1,500. It was an old beater that we kind of needed for our summer business but could do without. I had listed it at the end of the season in hopes of getting something nicer before next season. The lady came that day and paid us $1,500 in cash without haggling at all.

Rae and I felt God providing for us the whole way. We miraculously acquired the downpayment for our house. Surprisingly, I was able to negotiate moving into our new home a full month and a half before closing because it was vacant. I also negotiated not paying rent during this time. It was just enough time to move out of our old home and get a renter in there. We never made a double mortgage payment without rent income to provide the difference.

Biblical Reflection

Relying on God

Romans 8:32 "He who did not spare his own Son, but gave him up for us all—how will he not also, along with him, graciously give us all things?"

When God calls you into an impactful ministry it will not be easy. It will force you to rely on God. In doing so it will build your relationship with Christ. This means that you will go further with God than you have previously, leading into unknown territory. It is uncomfortable. If you have a clear vision from God and know His will, pray through every step. Stay close and seek the comfort of God. You will not be alone.

The problem many people take in executing God's will is attempting it solely by themselves. Do not forget, this is also God's mission. He is not a silent partner unless we force Him to be. He will help you along the way.

What physical hurdles are keeping you from God's mission for your life? Are you neglecting prayer? Do you have a clear vision for God's calling? What can you do about these things?

_____

_____

_____

_____

_____

_____

Prayer-

Jesus, help me to fully trust in you and follow through with Your calling for my life. Please make Your vision clear to me. Help me to keep You an active member in that calling. Make me aware of Your presence. -Amen

FALSE MEMORIES

THE WEEK WE MADE the down payment on our house we had $86 in our bank account until Rae got paid that weekend. Sweating bullets, we were budgeting the next three days of meals for six people. We knew pizza and spaghetti was in the future, but we could do it. In lieu of "good" pizza we were picking up a $5 special on Thursday when one of our kids threw a fit in the back of the car. I was appalled at this and couldn't imagine doing this to my parents. I was raised to eat what was served or I didn't eat at all.

The most absurd thing about it was knowing where they came from. Their file history went straight to my head. Just four years before they were literally eating food thrown to them on the floor by their parents, like they were cats. How could they forget this and become so ungrateful?

I was torn with emotion and just wanted to cry. I felt like I was doing all I could do for my children and was unappreciated. I literally had no money to get decent pizza that day, and I was also questioning the proper response that would address such rotten behavior.

A hard thing to acknowledge is that buying traumatized children anything they want will not make things better. Even adults have a tendency toward engaging in retail therapy when they feel low. If we are honest with ourselves, this is only a temporary band-aid. It is nothing but a distraction from what needs attention. We have all purchased that item we just had to have only to want something else shortly later.

Not long after this incident some of the kids got too rowdy and Rae put them in time out to settle them down. One of our other children piped up and said, "I miss our birth mom.". It is a moral struggle to hear this. It is important that your children don't see visually negative reactions to those statements. The last thing they need is for their adoptive parents to make them feel that their emotions are not valid or are ridiculous. However, it is important to know where those statements came from.

After discussing it further they divulged that they missed her because she never put them in timeout. Another piped in that she missed riding bikes at the house, which they never actually had. When coupling these situations together it is apparent that they were experiencing false memories.

The proper way to address this is argued by professionals in every direction possible. We settled on loving honesty. We cannot address this matter in a light that has our children forming false memories of their parents. It can be dangerous and cause them to suppress what truly happened or form a desired role model in their mind; what they wish their parents were. Or, how they wish they treated them.

Children need reality. They need to know why they are at our house and why their names were changed. They need to know that God has a place in their lives and that they are a gift. They have a lot to offer, and they need to know it. If our children falsely remember where they came from, they will forget to appreciate what they have.

Biblical Reflection

Forgetting God's Work

Judges 2:19 "But when the judge died, the people returned to ways even more corrupt than those of their

ancestors, following other gods and serving and worship-
ing them. They refused to give up their evil practices and
stubborn ways."

The Book of Judges follows a pattern of regression and a generation lost time and time again. This book drills down on the issue foster/adoptive families must end. A child lost in sin will have lost offspring. It creates the cycle of brokenness that God is calling us to end. Just as God sent a leader to the Israelites to direct them back to the true Creator, we are called to step in and end the generational sin with the child in our home.

A vital piece of ending this cycle is to remember what God has done for them. God guided you as a parent(s) to take them into a Christian home. They need to remember the grace God had on them, but not to dwell on it. Do not push your child into the past. God has a plan for their future. That cannot take place in the past.

-Prayer

Heavenly Father, guide me in the position You have put
me in. I cannot raise this child on my own. Help me be the
parent You are calling me to be. Let my child be receptive
to Your Word. Let them not forget the grace and mercy You
have shown them. -Amen

THE 3 STAGES OF PLACEMENT

THE ONLY WAY TO address these issues is through example. As a foster or adoptive parent, you must be consistent. If you say you are going to do something, follow through with it. If you are going to make an impact on your child(ren), you need to get to know them. You need to learn their "ticks" and interests. These are stepping-stones to building a relationship with them.

It seems that most people go through a phase in life where they feel they know more than their parents and they are immutable to the side-effects of being unwitting teenagers. Imagine you have a child come to you at seven or eight years old, and you are their fourth or fifth home.

The "typical" events that follow can be broken down into three stages. Stage One - Acclimation, they will likely be on good behavior for close to a month. This is partly because they personally want to settle down. They just came through a tough situation and all their belongings are in a few boxes or literal trash bags. They are scared, and perhaps embarrassed.

Their form of settling in is to observe you. They are taking note of your behavior and responses to situations. This child is measuring you up against their prior experiences. They are trying to take mental notes of what they can and cannot do in this new home.

You are now moving into Stage Two – Loyalty. Your child has likely not recovered from their loss. They lost their home(s), family, possibly moved school districts, likely neighborhoods. They have lost friends, family, and everything they have known.

In a child's mind, if they begin accepting you, they are giving up on their family and ever going back to their home and friends, what they know. They are going to try and be loyal to what they know is still out there. The process of attaching to their new family is also a grieving process and it likely won't be pretty.

After your child(ren) has acclimated to your home, they will begin testing their theories on your behavior. This could be through slowly letting their true colors show, or purposeful disruptions. They may begin spilling milk, clogging the toilet, swinging from kitchen cabinet doors, etc. Eventually, it can push further. If they are bored, or want to make you mad, they will see what your limits are.

After they have tested your responses, they will test your loyalty to them. They have been moved before. Whether it was from their biological parents, temporary placement, or another foster home; they have been taken from a permanent situation in their mind and have been emotionally hurt and let down.

When you start seeing this behavior contact a counselor experienced with "intensive placement stabilization". There are agencies that work with child and family services that help children attach to new foster families.

Some children are going to resist feeling comfortable with you. Again, if they allow themselves to attach to a new family it means a shift in loyalty. A grieving process will start for them. They are letting go of what could have been, or what they knew. They do not want to be hurt again. They are trying to protect themselves. Distrust has been ingrained into them. They do not trust that you are going to be their forever home. They want to resist being vulnerable again.

Think of this mindset like two junior high aged kids. Emma hears from her best friend that Nathan is going to break up with her at the end of the day. Emma can't bear the thought of someone breaking up with her. She does not want to feel rejected, so she preempts the rejection by rejecting Nathan first at lunch.

They are trying to see if you will ever give up on them. Some kids will begin trying unthinkable things to push your limits and see if you will give up on them.

The other side of this behavior, my wife and I have not personally experienced in significant depth, but some children feel they have personally done something wrong to be moved around from home to home. They may try to go above and beyond to get you to like them (i.e., cleaning up more than any child you have ever seen, serving you like a butler or maid, etc.). It can be easy to see some of this behavior in many "normal" children from time to time. However, just be careful with foster/adoptive children. Try to find out where the motivation is coming from. If they truly just have a servant's heart, great!

The Loyalty Stage is an emotional rollercoaster. Behaviors can blindside you, cause you to question your sanity. Manipulation, lies, and purposeful vendettas should be expected. There can, and likely will, be times when you may question why you ever disrupted a quiet "simple" life with unappreciated chaos.

In these moments it is important to know why you chose to foster or adopt. If you began this life-changing journey as the result of a call from the Lord, then you know you can get through it. If you chose to bring this child into your family because your friends were doing it, then you are in it for the wrong reason. If you signed on for this child because you thought it would be a nice thing to do, then you better begin pleading for help from God.

You will never be successful in spiritually impacting a child without the help of God. To think otherwise is illogical. Do not attempt this on your own. You are bringing a spiritual battle into your home. You better be in constant prayer over this child(ren), your home, and for God to guide you.

Adoption and foster care should never be taken lightly. The minute you take a child into your home you run the risk of further traumatizing the child you are trying to help and the rest of the members in your home.

Many families never make it past this stage. The reason for this is they simply address behaviors and not the cause of behaviors. Countless families flounder here in survival mode. They try to just get through the day with no issues and try to repeat the process the next day.

The problem is many families do not have the support or energy to take raising a child any further. Days may go by where it is all a foster parent can do not to make a call and have their child taken away for the sake of their own mental health. Or simply count the days until they are 18 years old.

If you are fostering a child and you begin feeling this way, ask for help. Look into respite care, or a family member or friend to give you a break. You need to find ways to get rejuvenated in every aspect of life. Plan for these breaks when you are preparing for your child placement. You will need to prepare to catch up on sleep and mental breaks.

If you maintain perseverance through Stage Two you will likely experience Stage Three - Transformation. Your child will have an emotional breakdown. When I say this, I do not necessarily mean a hospital stay emotional breakdown.

In Stage Three your child(ren) has realized you are there for them and they trust you. With this comes extreme emotion on their part. They have a realization that there is someone in their life they can depend on. You now could create a positive lasting effect on their life. It is important to maintain this trust. Be consistent, open yourself up to them. By doing this you are going to continue fostering a relationship that can run deeper than some biological relationships.

The reason I say this is that many people go through the motions of life and their child grows up. Be it the juggling between parents, possibly grandparents, based on work schedule. It is a common occurrence that children are only sat down in deep conversation when a problem arises. If you have a "well behaved child", or poor parenting skills, you may never have the push to foster a deep relationship with them. A solid bond may never occur.

If you crack through the rugged crust of history that tends to form around a foster child, then you can experience a truly rewarding relationship on both sides. If you make it past Stage Two you have the potential to be a voice that is heard which leads to ending the cycle of brokenness. You can lead them to the transformation only Christ can offer.

Biblical Reflection

The Commission

Matthew 28:18-20 "Then Jesus came to them and said, "All authority in heaven and on earth has been given to me. Therefore go and make disciples of all nations, baptizing them in the name of the Father and of the Son and of the Holy Spirit, and teaching them to obey everything I have commanded you. And surely I am with you always, to the very end of the age.""

The Great Commission is the universal call to every Christian. When someone states that they have a calling from God, the motive of that call should trace back to this set of verses. Spreading the Good News of Christ is what we are here for. We are not on earth to earn money for the latest sports car that is released. We are not on earth to play golf every weekend. Those are acceptable things to participate in, but does God want our lives to revolve around it?

About ten years ago I was getting ready for bed. Rae was asleep across the house, and I popped a vitamin in my mouth. I immediately began to choke. I became terrified and thought, *Seriously God? I haven't even started on the calling you have for me!* I found a chair and slammed my gut into the back of it popping the pill out. Gasping for air I thought, it's time to figure out what God is calling me to do with my life.

Every day that passes by means Jesus is one day closer to returning. We are not promised tomorrow. Are you wasting your time? What is God's calling for your life?

Making Time

TIME, THE ONE THING all of humanity is regulated by. So much is crammed into our lives we rarely do anything to the best of our ability. Expectations are high when breaking down our hours in a day. Tasks fight for your time. House projects, broken toys, and a messy work desk fall to the bottom of the pile as the workload continually grows. If you are like me, you get to work between 7-7:30 am and work through lunch. After getting home between 5-6:00 pm you finish up emails and computer work. At that point Rae or I would help manage our other business that was open until 9-10 pm. I would get a little sleep and start it over the next day.

After adoption and our surprise baby, we struggled with time management. Rae was running her business getting supplies, dropping them off at all the locations, and opening those locations with five children in tow. She had little down time. I am a borderline workaholic to begin with and I don't want to be. There have been times I worked until 1-2:00 am and got up at 5:00 am to go to work. I think it is important occasionally to step back and look at your life. Lay out your day and ask three questions. Is it a sustainable life for you and your family? Will it get you where you want to be in five years or ten years? Above all, is this what God wants you to do?

When we were first married, Rae and I were helping each other grow our businesses to develop a future for ourselves. This worked well and we were cautious not to become addicted to the work or that carrot dangling in front of us. For most people as they start a family they slowly dial back "all the things". When our immediate transition to a large family happened, we had a shock to reality. I likely alienated some people by removing myself from several bands I played with on the weekends, but I found myself literally working myself sick at times. The ultimate question came, "What do we do?". Kids are expensive. Summer camps almost require a second mortgage, not to mention the monthly food bill! Those concerns confront you before thinking about family time.

We obviously need to work to support our family, but is it right to watch reality shows from 7-9:00pm and talk to your child for only 10 minutes a night? Another concerning fact is one-third of couples spend less than 30 minutes together each day. With a divorce rate over 50 percent, where are we dedicating our time? (UK, 2011)

I had an eye-opening day during my busy season at work. I went to work before anyone was up and when I got home everyone was in bed. That hit me hard. I had not seen my baby's smile all day. I had not hugged any of my children. I did not have much of a conversation with Rae either. It would have been different had I been on a business trip, but I was thinking this was not too different of a day. Typically, Rae would run by our store, and I could see the kids, but it was just too busy that day.

I am not sure if it was that week or the next week someone approached us wanting to buy our summer business. I could not get the need for family time out of my head when we sat down to discuss this. This was a big deal for us. The business made decent money and was almost paid off. Sitting in negotiations over the purchase, I felt like God was handing us family time. We made the deal and have not looked back. We took that step back and looked at where our family was and where we would be in five to ten years. All I saw was my children grown up and me vacant from noticing.

One of the most important things a parent can do is be there. Be present. When you are having "family time" with your kids "be there", put the phone down. Kids notice everything parents are doing. If we fail to show them as a priority, they will take notice. Hug your kids and talk with them. Tell them you love them. Show them they are loved with your time.

As a parent and Christian, the most important thing you can do with your child is to raise them to love Christ and be part of God's Kingdom. It is hard to do that without spending time with them.

It just happened that time was needed in our life more than we were aware. All our children have an Individualized Education Plan (IEP) at school. These plans were put in place for delayed learning. Over the period of a few years communicating with different specialists, we were confronted with the knowledge that our youngest son did not just have a delay in learning. He had a low IQ level.

This made me feel a little sick to my stomach. I believed he was just a little slow coupled with a delay in learning, but it was more serious. After having the tests explained to me, I felt like I had been too hard on him over the past few years. My standards for him were higher than he could meet. Many of the behaviors he exhibits are outside of his control.

That evening Rae and I sat down our older children and explained to them that we needed to take a different approach to his behaviors and needs. He is not just being lazy at times. He is going to need some extra help in general. During that conversation you could tell that our kids truly look out for each other. They were completely understanding and showed genuine concern.

It is important to be aware of this possibility when adopting. You do not always know genetic history. For us, this knowledge would not have played a role in our decision to adopt. He is our child, and we love him. However, depending on the manner that you adopt, you can negotiate medical assistance into the adoption. That could have been beneficial for us had we known. Some of the opportunities we would like to have taken advantage of are not covered by insurance and come out of pocket. This is important to keep in mind.

Before you adopt a child from foster care try to get any testing done that you may be curious about. It could help your child down the road to be able to take part in opportunities that may be beyond your financial reach.

Biblical Reflection

Ideal Family – Adam and Eve

In the beginning God created His ideal model of a family. Many times, we get caught up in comparing lifestyles and the next thing we could do that would make our life better. The reality is that our role in the family is tailored by society. If we take a step back and compare our role to God's example for us it is going to trace back to Adam and Eve. Before sin was in this world God created something so perfect that once sin entered in, the garden was shut off from the world. Our example of an ideal model should come from the garden.

In the garden Adam and Eve experienced God walking among them. Adam was not tied down to back breaking work. Eve did not flirt with sin. Their life was good when they stayed close to God.

What are some areas of your life that could change to be more like the garden? Do you tie yourself down to work more than is necessary? Do unnecessary pressures of society get in the way of a stronger relationship with God and your family?

_____

_____

_____

_____

_____

_____

Prayer-

Heavenly father, give me the strength to remove things from my life that may be hindering my growth in You. Give me the courage to reach out for help and accountability in changing my life toward a stronger relationship with You. Help me to lead my family by example. -Amen

Do Something

ON ANY GIVEN DAY, there are nearly 438,000 children in foster care in the United States. In 2016, over 687,000 children spent time in U.S. foster care. On average, children remain in state care for nearly two years and six percent of children in foster care have languished there for five or more years (Children's Rights, 2023).

There are 107,918 foster children eligible for and waiting to be adopted. In 2014, 50,644 foster kids were adopted — a number that has stayed roughly consistent for the past five years. The average age of a waiting child is 7.7 years old and 29% of them will spend at least three years in foster care (Adoption Network, 2023).

These numbers are tough to read. There are close to 700,000 children who come from situations so bad that they were removed from their homes. Forget the family that you view as too strict in the grocery line. Ignore the family that yells at their kids in the restaurant and makes a scene. These kids were either: physically or sexually abused, starved, severely neglected, influenced by drugs, or all the above. These are the kids out there who need loved and exposed to a Christian atmosphere.

Countless studies show children in foster care exposed to a loving home for six months or longer in their lifetime are drastically more likely to have a successful relationship when they grow up. It is hard to place a value on that. There is potential to help a child and break the cycle of brokenness. There is potential to stop Satan's work in its tracks.

Adoption and foster care are Biblical. Moses was adopted, Joseph raised Jesus, Samuel was given back to God at the temple. Ruth was not an Israelite but was adopted into the lineage of Jesus. The list goes on and on.

The numbers above indicate that there are around 57,000 children who need to be adopted from foster care. There are around 100,000 churches in America. If one out of two churches adopted a child, we would be taking care of the kids needing a home.

I am proud to come from a church where I know there are around 40 kids who have been adopted. God calls us to take care of one another. We are taught to have compassion. We are bound by the Ten Commandments to treat others the way we would want to be treated. All of this adds to a conviction among Christians.

Pastor Francis Chan once explained that he feels God wants us to adopt children into our families unless He calls us not to. This is an interesting concept. I do not completely disagree or agree with that statement. If you are a Christian, then you should be in prayer about God's calling for your life. Through regular prayer that question should be realized. Every Christian should be in prayer about God's call for their life. Adoption should be part of that.

If a child was left on your front step, would you leave him or her in the rain? You would take them inside and call the police. If later that night they couldn't find a home and you could keep them at your house, would you? In the area I live they are having to shuttle kids up to Chicago to an orphanage because there are not enough foster homes. When I hear about that news I want to cry. That could have been our kids.

During the process of our adoption Rae brought up the significance of our suffering and God's timing during our miscarriage. The same month we miscarried, our children were pulled from their biological homes and placed in foster care. Had I not heard God's call to sign up for foster care or promptly responded to His will we never would have experienced the joy they have brought to our home. I personally would never would have been able to have baptized three of my children who proclaimed Jesus as their Savior. They may never have been saved. They would likely have remained in separate home, probably three different ones.

Listen to God, follow Jesus, and seek the Holy Spirit. One of the greatest things a Christian family can do is take a child into their home and teach them about Christ. Be part of God's plan.

Biblical Reflection

God's Will– *Deuteronomy 10:18 "He executes justice for the fatherless and the widow, and loves the sojourner, giving him food and clothing."*

The context of this verse is inspiring. In a time where the Israelites had left the pagan home of Egypt, God was trying to develop a relationship with them. He was trying to show his character. To illustrate this, he explains that he will stand up for those in need. He will give them food and clothing.

As Christians, we are called to be extensions of Christ. We are called to give food and clothing to those in need. We can let Christ be seen in us by showing compassion to those in need. God is a father to the fatherless (Psalms 68:5). Are we doing God's will if we fail to put our faith into action? The scariest verse in the Bible for me is Matthew 7:21 "Not everyone who says to me, 'Lord, Lord', will enter the kingdom of heaven, but only the one who does the will of my Father who is in heaven." What is God's will for you? Are you preparing for it?

Bibliography

Forbes Magazine. (2023, September 4). *Mental health statistics.* Forbes. https://www.forbes.com/health/mind/mental-health-statistics/#:~:text=Anxiety%20disorders%20grew%20from%20about,50%20and%20over%20(14.5%25).

Key facts and statistics. National Foster Care Month - Child Welfare Information Gateway. (n.d.). https://www.childwelfare.gov/fostercaremonth/awareness/facts/

Rights of youth in Foster Care. Rights of Youth in Foster Care - Child Welfare Information Gateway. (2023, January). https://www.childwelfare.gov/topics/systemwide/youth/resourcesforyouth/rights-of-youth-in-foster-care/

Sbrown@casey.org. (2023, June 23). *Placement stability impacts.* Casey Family Programs. https://www.casey.org/placement-stability-impacts/#:~:text=The%20trauma%20that%20accompanies%20placement,aggression%2C%20delinquency%2C%20and%20depression.&text=Multiple%20placements%20have%20also%20been,and%20challenges%20developing%20meaningful%20attachments.

Sosiladmin. (2022, November 9). *SOS Illinois focuses on adoption for children in Foster Care.* SOS Children's Villages Illinois. https://www.sosillinois.org/sos-illinois-recognizes-national-adoption-awareness-month-a-story-you-need-to-hear/#:~:text=Foster%20Care%20and%20Adoption%20

Statistics%20and%20Facts&text=With%20nearly%20 450%2C000%20children%20in,are%20waiting%20to%20 be%20adopted

Study highlights long-term benefits of family-based care following insti-tutional care. Psychiatry.org - Study Highlights Long-Term Benefits of Family-Based Care Following Institutional Care. (2023, May 22). https://www.psychiatry.org/News-room/ News-Releases/Study-Highlights-Benefits-of-Family-Based-Care#:~:text=Children%20who%20remained%20 with%20other,in%20outcomes%20measured%20in%20 adolescence.

UK, T. H. P. (2011, November 30). *British couples only spend 30 minutes a day together.* HuffPost UK. https://www.huff-ingtonpost.co.uk/2011/11/30/couples-spend-just-30-minutes-a-day-together_n_1120721.html?guce_refer-rer_us=aHR0cHM6Ly93d3cuZ29vZ2xlLmNvLnphLw&gu ce_referrer_cs=k9fkcNNycr4hmxDHjX-nPA

US Adoption Statistics: Adoption Network. Adoption Network |. (2023, March 22). https://adoptionnetwork.com/ adoption-myths-facts/domestic-us-statistics/

www.ingramcontent.com/pod-product-compliance
Lightning Source LLC
LaVergne TN
LVHW041201080426
835511LV00006B/696